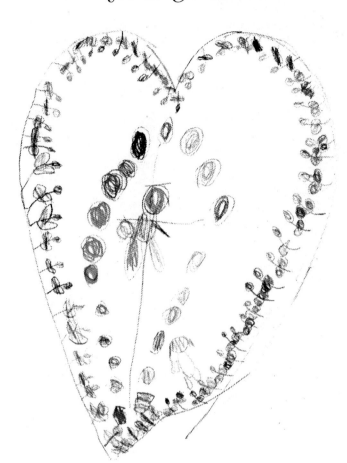

by the Children of the
Rutherford County
Boys & Girls Clubs

Write Together™ Publishing
Nashville, TN

Published by Write Together Publishing ™ LLC.
www.writetogether.com

ISBN   1-931718-11-3 Paperback

Title: Giving is...
Subject: Children's Literary Collections

Project Coordinator: Ralph Vaughn
Cover Art: Shelby Givens

For Write Together Publishing:

Publisher: Paul Clere

Edit: John D. Bauman

Book Design: Bill Perkins

To publish a book for your school or non-profit organization that complements
your academic goals or values, vision and mission, please contact:

Write Together ™ Publishing
533 Inwood Dr.
Nashville, TN 37211

phone: 615-781-1518
fax: 520-223-4850
www.writetogether.com

Table of Contents

Foreword

Giving is an overall expression of a caring heart. I am proud of the children at our Boys & Girls Clubs for contributing to this project.

As you read their words about giving, I am sure that you will see the kind of values taught at the Club. I have been personally touched by their expressions. I know you will be touched, too.

Our goal at the Boys & Girls Clubs is to encourage the children to embrace and express values that will take them further in life as productive, responsible and caring citizens.

This book is a gift from the children at the Club to each other, to the community, and to anyone looking for a treasure today... and years from now.

Leigh Huddleston
President

Chapter One
Poetry

Art by Lauren Walker

Giving is good
Giving is great
Giving makes me
Feel good inside
Lindsey Davenport, Age 11
Christine Jarrett, Age 11

Cookies are good, cookies are sweet,
Cookies are something you could eat.
Give me chocolate chips sprinkled on top.
It is something good to eat
Dallas Brobst, Age 11

Giving is good.
Giving is great.
Giving is what
God creates.
Sareda Calderon, Age 11

Giving is...

I give love to my dog
I give money to my mom
I give presents to my family
I give my life to God
Cody Bragg, Age 10

Greatness
Idealness
Victory
Important
Never ending
Gladness
Giving fills our hearts with joy.
Tamyra Bradby (Miss Tamyra), Staff

I give them clothes
I give them gifts
I give them laughter
I give them love
I give and share all
My things
I give them all my love
I give them all my jokes
Jesus gave his life
I am trying to do the same
For my family and all
My friends.
Chelsee Barbo, Age 13

Giving is special to those who care for you
For when you're down I'll be around
For you to tell your problems to.
I'll be there in a second flat if you are in need,
And I'll always be there when you call.
For giving is special to those who care
For you and me,
I know you'll be there for me in my time of need
And I'll be there for you because giving is
Special to me like no other one!
Jenna Ladd, Age 13

I love to give
Giving is good
Giving is neat
If you like to give, you are very sweet
So give to people in need
Amanda Simons, Age 11

Giving is the beggin'. Of coming back for seconds.
Don't hate because I'm not giving you bling bling.
Money ain't a thang. I'm not trying to make
You a wannabe. The next day you be walkin'
In looking like sisquo and looking right ghetto.
See that's why I'm not giving you my dough.
Ashley Johnson, Age 12

Giving is to share, to help someone in need
Giving is to love, to give your love to people, to show them
    you care
Giving is helping others less fortunate than others
Giving helps the world to grow
Giving can do wonders
Giving can make friendships
Giving is what I'm doing
Giving is what I see
Every time you turn and look
Someone is giving.
Courtney Kershaw, Age 13

Giving is a nice thing to do
Whenever someone gives something to you!
Halee Gregory, Age 9

Giving is...

When I go outside every day
I sometimes give away.
Just like I like to live,
I like to give.
Kyle Goolesby, Age 11

Giving is nice.
Giving is like rice.
Giving is like ice.
I like giving because it's cool!
Jasmine Goolesby, Age 9

Giving
Giving is
Giving is good
Giving is good and
Giving is good and nice
Giving is good and nice for
Giving is good and nice for everyone!
Adrian Rippy, Age 13

When I am giving
I feel real good.
I give lots of things
Because I know I should.
Giving is the best.
Why don't you give everything
And even the rest?
Austin Richardson, Age 13

Giving is a very special thing.
It's loving, caring, you can even sing
To the elderly and give presents to the poor
And you will love it so much.
You'll give more and more.
Olivia Preston, Age 12

To give from the heart
Makes me feel like
GOLD.
I love to give.
I love the way it makes
Me feel.
Keywannia Pickett, Age 13

Giving is good all the time.
It really starts to blow my mind.
Every time I give away,
I never have anything to say.
But giving is fun to me.
That's the way life should be.
Mike Oden, Age 13

Good, sweet
It's nice to give
Very nice and sweet
It is good to give
Nice
Great to give
Amanda Simons, Age 11

If I give to someone,
Someone gives back.
But if someone needs it,
I don't need anything back.
Giving is fun.
Giving is good.
Giving helps everyone around.
Giving makes me feel good.
Chelsee Barbo, Age 13

Roses are red,
Violets are blue,
Giving is what
Girls and boys do.
Michael Moore, Age 11

Giving is...

Giving is a nice thing to do
For people that aren't as fortunate as me and you.
I love to give because it is right.
People should love to give because God gave us life.
Through giving you can touch peoples' life as well as your own.
So I thought this would be a great little poem.
Emil Mitchell (Mr. Emil), Staff

Giving is good.
Giving is great.
If you give you get thanked.
So give, give, give and you are great!
Liqa Minter, Age 12

I give to you
That is very nice
I give to you
That's just right
Alicia Todd, Age 8

Grateful
Incredible
Very nice
Intellectual
Noticeable
Good
Amanda Manning, Age 13

I share a ball.
I share a bat.
I share a base.
Drew Woods, Age 7

I feel happy to give to others.
I like it when people give.
I helped my aunt walk.
My friend had no friends so we talk.
Michael Moore, Age 11

If you don't like to give, that's very mean.
If you'd like to give, that's neat.
We like to give.
So, if we like to give,
It's really great, really neat, really is the best.
It can't be beat!
Jessica Williams, Age 11

Give to everybody!
I love giving!
Vets help give birth to baby animals.
I think everyone should give.
No one should be mean.
Giving is very good.
Kayla Walker, Age 9

I give and receive
I play and I need
I help and I pray
One day, some day
Everyone will
Be okay.
Olivia Preston, Age 12

G is for *God*, who loves me very much.
I is for *intelligence*, which teachers give to me.
V is for *valuable*, which is what my family is.
I is for *independence*, which I have earned.
N is for *nice*, which is how all my friends are.
G is for *good*, which is what my life has been like!
Adrian Rippy, Age 13

Giving is...

God gave to us.
If God gave, you should give.
Very great to do.
In the beginning of a friendship you give.
Nice to others by giving them something.
Graceful to others.
Keywannia Pickett, Age 13

Giving is about life and rules.
Maybe I have many tools.
Around the world is good for me.
Glory is for all of thee.
Mike Oden, Age 13

G is for giving
I love to give
V is for being very nice
I love to give to my family
Never ask for something back
Giving is great
Savannah Tarpley, Age 9

Giving
Is fun and
Very cool.
It's
Nice and
Great.
Jake Tarpley, Age 10

Giving is a good thing.
Giving is a nice thing.
Giving is what you do.
Giving is what you get.
I like to give things to other people.
People like giving to me.
That is what giving is.
Samantha Spencer, Age 14

Good
Inspiring
Valentine
Everyone
Jessica Simons, Age 8

People give all sorts of kinds.
You should be really kind.
I would give to a friend of mine.
We should give all the time.
If you give you'll get a hand,
So we should give all the time.
Amanda Simons, Age 11

I shared my balls.
I shared my dolls.
I shared with friends.
I'll share to the end.
Cameron Watkins, Age 7

Giving is very nice.
Giving is like ice.
Giving is like mice.
Giving is a fight.
Giving is the morning light.
Giving is like the dark night.
Alex Scott, Age 9

Giving is what people do
Giving is what we should do
Giving is very nice
Just like sugar and spice.
Michael Moore, Age 11

Giving is...

One day I received a gift
That came from above.
It's better than toys or clothes,
It's better than ribbons or bows.
It's the gift of love.
And as I said before,
It's sent from above
Lauren Walker, Age 12

Giving is good.
Giving is cool.
Giving is something
We all love to do
Adrian Rippy, Age 13

When I give, I feel good.
You should give, you know you should.
If you could give every day,
Just give, give, give away.
You should give, you know you should,
'Cause when you give it makes you feel good.
Amanda Simons, Age 11

Violets are red,
Some flowers are blue.
Nothing else is sweeter
Than giving to you.
Alicia Todd, Age 8

When
Giving is from the heart,
Not a store or mall,
Giving is the greatest gift
Greatest gift of all.
And that's all.
Amanda Simons, Age 11

What a wonderful, giving Earth we live in.
It provides for us in so many ways...
It spins creating night and day.
It gives you food and seeds to grow.
It also gives you great things to climb on.
It supplies water and love.
We have stars and clouds.
Life—we should recycle to show we care and stop pollution.
Jessica Simons, Age 8
Heather Currey, Age 6
Cody Maynard, Age 7
William Leach, Age 8
Joe Ramirez, Age 7
Booker Leach, Age 6
Keelea Fults, Age 8
Sammie Bell, Age 7
Alicia Todd, Age 8
Brandon Dunn, Age 8
Kalesha Johnson, Age 7
Leeah Turner, Age 6
Curronica Lowery, Age 6
Tra Norwood, Age 7
Stephen Duke, Age 7
Sharie Moore, Age 7

Giving is great.
Giving is good.
Thank you for giving.
Amen
Adrian Rippy, Age 13

Giving is...

We give hope, we give love,
We give it our all.
We give knowledge, we give strength,
We give friendship that lasts a lifetime.
We give without receiving.
We give things without even knowing it.
And we should rejoice in knowing
We give.
Lauren Walker, Age 12

I like to give.
I like to live.
I like to have fun.
I like to run.

Giving is fun
Like I like to run.
I like to give
Like I live.

Living is fun.
Giving is fun.
I like to run.
I like to have fun.

I like to be good at giving
Just like I would like living.
I like to do good
Like I saw wood.
Kyle Goolesby, Age 11

Chapter Two
Boys & Girls Club

Art by Brooke Duke

The Boys & Girls Club gives.
It gives to all the kids.
It helps all the moms and dads
By watching all the girls and lads.
The Boys & Girls Club gives all the time.
It gives to all the friends of mine.
Amanda Simons, Age 11

Our gifts are great,
But what we give is better.
We give our trust and our friendship.
We give to our community
And we get what we give back.
We as a Club are very gracious
To all the people we give to.
Lauren Walker, Age 12

Giving is...

The Boys & Girls Club has given me courage to make friends.
Christian Johnson, Age 9

The Boys & Girls Club is really cool.
I love it so much, I follow the rules.
They built it by stone and brick.
They built it very quick, quick, quick.
And I am thankful very much
For giving the very loving touch.
Jordan Davis, Age 9

What is giving to me? I think that it is when you give to someone that needs it or as a gift. Giving is whatever you want to think it is, but what I said is what I think it is. When I give, I feel like it can and will help someone or something. If the kids at the Boys & Girls Club like to give, you should too!
Jeff Davis, Age 9

Mr. John makes the very best snacks for all of us. His chocolate chip cookies are so delicious and yummy. He gets the food and cooks because we don't know how. He does this every day for everyone in the whole Club.

One day Mr. John went to a lady's house and moved a big heavy shelf so he could connect her Nintendo, and he did it free.

One day Mr. John kept me busy and out of trouble and let me help him clean up the Club.

One day Mr. John took me to the playground because I was lost and couldn't find my group. He made me feel safe.
Joe Ramirez, Age 7
Cody Martin, Age 7
Savannah Casterline, Age 7
Sara Hayes, Age 7
Michael Wigfall, Age 7

The Boys & Girls Club gave me friends, love, two playgrounds, a place to play basketball, a gym, games room, the learning resource center, and the best place to go after school.
Brooke Duke, Age 9

The Club takes me on field trips. They give me lots of fun. The Club helps me.
Jeff Davis, Age 9

They give me a bumper ball set.
They give me a snack.
They give me activities.
They let me have fun,
And they give me other fun stuff to do.
Justin Currey, Age 11

Roses are red,
Violets are blue.
Boys & Girls Club
Is the best giving place for you!
Melissa Cameron, Age 13

The Boys & Girls Club gives just like we give to them in our lives. Boys & Girls Club gives back to us and we give to them.
Chris Bush, Age 12

The Boys & Girls Club is a wonderful place to be because they teach us how to be honest, self-respecting, responsible, and respectful of Club property. If I owned $5,000, I would be soooo nice to give it *all* to the Boys & Girls Club.
John Bucy, Age 10

The Boys & Girls Club gave me food, a game room, and a basketball net and court. And they have cool staff.
Devon Brown, Age 9

I would feel good and happy to give to the Boys & Girls Club. I would probably give something to Mr. Steve because he is nice and understanding.
Dallas Brobst, Age 11

Giving is...

The Boys & Girls Club has given me games to play. They give me snacks. They have given me a place to go after school and a place to play basketball.
Anastasia Brobst, Age 9

The Boys & Girls Club has given me a membership card, snacks, and a magazine. They gave me fun and a shirt and took me swimming and skating.
Cody Bragg, Age 9

The United Way helps our dreams come true by giving money to our Club.
Kacey Blackburn, Age 10

They Boys & Girls Club gave me care. They gave me fun and a snack.
Zack Ashburn, Age 8

Giving is what the Boys & Girls Club does for us kids. They give us a place to go and hang out. We get skills from some of the things we do. The Club is the positive place for kids.
Chaisson Allen, Age 12

The Club gives me fun and makes me happy. The Boys & Girls Club rocks!
Sam Loyd, Age 8

The Boys & Girls Club gives me a computer lab, and a table and chairs where I can sit and do my homework. And Mr. John gives us cookies for snack.
Katie Lower, Age 11

Roses are red,
Violets are blue.
The Boys & Girls Club
Is the best giving place ever!
Melissa Lee, Age 13

The Boys & Girls Club gave me a place to have fun, go on field trips, and more fun stuff.
Marquise Lawrence, Age 9

The Boys & Girls Club gave me a place to come after school, and a gym and gameroom.
Silvestre Juarez, Age 9

I like to give and never receive.
Coming to the Club means a lot to me.
I'm giving breath every day.
I can say, giving is the way.
Ashley Johnson, Age 12

The Boys & Girls Club gave me courage, my spirit, and my soul.
Julia Jones, Age 9

I give my time to Ms. Connie at the Boys & Girls Club. I help her in the learning resource center. I put up books and organize video games, the book shelf, and the CD's. I like giving help to Ms. Connie because she enjoys my company. I like giving. It makes me happy.
Alex Johnson, Age 14

The Boys & Girls Club is the best place I could be because the staff are nice to me. Mr. John gives us free snacks, and we get to do fun things like be in the gameroom or play in the gym. They let us do our homework here and they help us too.
Christine Jarrett, Age 11

Giving is...

The Boys & Girls Club gave me friends and gave me a place to go. I hope the Club stays forever.
Zach Jackson, Age 9

The Boys & Girls Club has given me a place to go after school and the chance to play baseball when I thought I had missed it.
Eric Hughes, Age 9

The Boys & Girls Club
Gave me a hope, a home, and a friend to turn to
Gave me love, then more love
Gave me a free place to go
Gave a lot of sleepovers
And girlfriends
Gave me things I can't forget
Brandon Herman, Age 13

The Boys & Girls Club gives me cheer. The Club is a very big place. The Boys & Girls Club is cool.
Tyler Hall, Age 7

The Boys & Girls Club is fun and great. It's a place to go for fun and play. Come on, let's go today!
Halee Gregory, Age 9

I love to give because I live to help people. I am happy that people gave to the Boys & Girls Club or I would not be able to come here. The Boys & Girls Club has given me a lot. They gave me a place to come after school, a place to meet new people and friends. That means a lot to me. I hope that it stays open because I really like the Boys & Girls Club.
Hillary Garrett, Age 9

The Boys & Girls Club gives
Just like they all live.
They give help to the community,
And the community raises money for the Club.
Kyle Goolesby, Age 11

First of all, I would like to thank Mr. Steve for being our director. The Boys & Girls Club is a place for kids to fellowship with each other. It is a place where we can get help on homework and get it done.
Chaisson Allen, Age 12

It is a good place to be.
It provides transportation for kids.
It is fun and somewhere to chill.
I like the Boys & Girls Club.
Dallas Brobst, Age 11

The Club gives me...
A snack
My books
A place to play
A place to meet new friends.
E'stasha Garrett, Age 9

Mr. Derek is very nice. I like him a lot. He explains things for me. He gives me ideas and tells me how to be respectful and responsible.
Taylor Rutland, Age 9

The Club gave me friendship, trust, and free time.
Stephen Price, Age 9

Giving is...

Mr. John gave me a snack to eat, because I gave the Boys & Girls Club money so he could buy the snacks we eat. I felt happy about that.
Marquise Lawrence, Age 9

The Boys & Girls Club gave me a place to go. It gave me friends. I gave a kid here a quarter because I wanted to.
Zach Jackson, Age 9

The Club gives the kids transportation from school, and when they give us things, we give things back. They gave me my life, my air, my inner soul. And in return, I gave them my honesty.
John Bucy, Age 10

The Boys & Girls Club gave me friends and supported me in a lot of ways.
Jacob Price, Age 10

Mr. Emil gives me help with my homework. Mr. John gives me a snack. I give my mom flowers. My mom gives me love. My grandma gives me food. My brother gives me Pokémon cards.
Devon Brown, Age 9

If people gave more, it would be a better place. Just the other day the Boys & Girls Club received a lot of school supplies for us kids. I think that can help. I am thankful.
Hillary Garret, Age 9

They gave me respect and I respect that. I think this place is great. I want to come here every day.
Austin Poteete, Age 8

The Boys & Girls Club has given me a fun place to stay in the summer and in the school year. I thank them very much.
Emily Parsley, Age 8

One day, Mr. John found my card when I lost it. He did not charge me for a new one.

He helps keep the Club very clean for all of us. He cleans up after us when we get sick.

When someone broke the toilet with a rock this summer, he cleaned the terrible mess for us.

It's real nice when Mr. John gives us pops, cookies, and bubble gum.

At the end of the day, he is very tired, and he goes home to help take care of his mother and brother. And every day he does it all again.

He is a very loyal and dependable staff member at the Boys & Girls Club. He sets a good example for all the kids at the Club.

If we didn't have Mr. John in our lives, we would be miserable.
Sam Loyd, Age 8
Tori Hughes, Age 6
Shelby Givens, Age 6
Nathan Gill, Age 6
Jonathan Maynard, Age 7
Sara Hayes, Age 7

Boys & Girls Club is about being positive. It means presents and a gift.
Mike Oden, Age 13

At Boys & Girls Club they gave me two Boys & Girls Club shirts. One was purple and it has my name on it now.
Stevie Moore, Age 9

Mr. John gives me an afternoon snack.
Randi Moore, Age 10

The Boys & Girls Club gave me the privilege to have fun.
Cody Martin, Age 7

Giving is...

I want to thank the Boys & Girls Club for giving me field trips and snacks. The B&GC gives to the community and provides a place for kids so they won't be at home eating and sleeping and watching TV. They can have a fun place to play and go on field trips like bowling and skating. Maybe once in a year they let us have a sleepover. I like to come to the B&GC because I like to help and give my free time to play with the children and help them in any way that I can.
Liqa Minter, Age 12

The Boys & Girls Club gave care and food and they helped me learn. I love the Boys & Girls Club.
Nicole Maynard, Age 8

People give all the time, but some people don't take the time to notice. They just take it for granted. I wish people would realize it as it happens. I have gotten a lot of things, and I hope the Boys & Girls Club gets a lot of things so that it can stay open. I want my kids to go there when they get older because I really enjoy it.
Hillary Garrett, Age 9

The Boys & Girls Club gave me a place to go after school instead of having to stay at home all by myself. It gives me the chance to meet new people and even make new friends.
DeAndrea Mack, Age 12

I'm proud that the Boys & Girls Club has given me a place to stay after school. I live in Murfreesboro and my name is Drew. I am proud that I have a house. I am proud that my mom can cook good food. And thanks for all these things.
Drew Woodard, Age 8

Giving is important because you feel good and other people feel good. You might feel sad or mad, but it makes you happy. Ms. Angel gave me candy and I give her love. Thank you, Boys & Girls Club.
Jessica Simons, Age 8

Giving is good. The Boys & Girls Club likes to give. They gave me a pair of skates for my birthday, and that was fun. I gave my brother a pair of pants today and a watch, and that was love.
Travis Whiteman, Age 11

The Boys & Girls Club gives me a better way to look at things. This place lets me be with my friends and be in a good environment at the same time. I really appreciate the things that the club does for people, such as giving them a good place to stay during the afternoon times. The Boys & Girls Club helps children with a bad attitude recognize that they shouldn't be mean to other people and that they're not the only people in the world that they should care about. I think for the most part the Boys & Girls Club has a big effect on everyone's life once you decide to join as a member.

The Club has given me a "shoulder to cry on" whenever I needed someone to talk to. I think that a lot of people take the Club for granted. A lot of people also would like to join but can't.

The Boys & Girls Club has given me a lot of good memories that I can always cherish.

I thank God for giving us all such a wonderful place.
Jessica Walls, Age 13

Boys & Girls Club – They gave me love.
Kayla Walker, Age 9

Boys & Girls Club loves to give. So we all need to give so everybody is happy. Giving is very neat and very sweet.
Jessica Williams, Age 11

Making Snacks
My reason for making cookies each day is to make the kids (and the staff) feel good. This past summer, I baked over 10,000 cookies (that's 300-350 a day!). Some of the kids helped me make the cookies because they know how nice I really am to them. I really love them from the bottom of my heart because they know how hard I work each day.

23

Giving is...

The strange thing about this is that God works in strange and mysterious ways, and I figured He would help me too. I'd never baked anything in my life. In high school I nearly failed home economics, and I had to learn how to cook through other sources.

Cleaning the Club

Before I became the Snack Man, my main job was (and still is) to keep the Boys & Girls Club clean.

Each day since January 1998, I come in to see what I have to do each day. I vacuum the floors, clean and sanitize the bathrooms, and sometimes wipe windows and repair stuff that's been broken.

The great thing about cleaning is that the kids get involved in this too. It makes them feel good because they know they can help me out each day in the snack room and other parts of the building that I am involved with. Don't forget, Jesus plays a part in this role too.

Bell Ringing for the Salvation Army

The sounds of Christmas are upon us—parades, parties, and the best thing, gifts. But what about the less fortunate? Well, that's where the Salvation Army comes in.

Each Christmas, since 1986, I have been a bell ringer for the organization, raising more than $2 million to help those in need of Christmas. I have rung bells in Columbia, Franklin, Tullahoma, Smyrna, Lebanon, and selected stores around Murfreesboro before I was positioned at my ringing post in K-Mart, now Big K-Mart, in 1991.

Once again, it makes the kids in our community feel good because our Club members got involved by visiting me over the holidays to see how I was doing (especially in 25° weather).

But guess what? I didn't give up because God was on my side too. He guided and protected me through all of the elements of Christmas bell ringing.

Organizing

One of my first jobs I ever did when I was hired at the Boys & Girls Club was organizing. At the time I didn't know how to do it; but as time went on, I took the time to think about what goes where and which is which.

Setups

It all began on January 5, 1999, when the Rotary Club met at the Club. My job was to set up 120 Rotarians for Tuesdays and 60 for Thursday breakfast. It took me from 4 to 8 months to figure out how to set up right. Once again the kids helped in this too. It made them feel good because the good Lord up above was included in this too. Isn't it amazing how Jesus is a mind regulator, a lawyer in the courtroom, and a doctor in the sick room?

Community Service Volunteers (CSV)

This segment has been helpful. Since 1999 there have been a total of 60+ CSV's. Some were former Club members, the others were brushing the laws of nature. From ages 12-35, I have led a total of 30 CSV's to complete their hours, ranging from 4 to 200 hours in a short period of time.

It made them feel good because they know they made a mistake; and because of God, they have faith in themselves not to do it again. Some CSV's went on to get jobs, some finished their school duties. Even one visited the Club this summer to thank me for what I gave her.

Finally, my reason for giving is because the kids are wonderful, God is good to me, and also, if it hadn't been for the Boys & Girls Club, I would have been in a whole lot of trouble. God bless you, and may He forever keep you.
John Verge (Mr. John), Staff

The Boys & Girls Club has given me time to do softball and other things. They also let you do your homework and get help. They have lots of fun games and sports.
Nikki Trice, Age 13

The Boys & Girls Club is very good. I like the Boys & Girls Club because it gives us stuff and food and takes us places. It teaches us how to give too.
Alicia Todd, Age 8

Giving is...

What the Boys & Girls Club gave me was trips to Sports*COM to swim, and then to go skating. They also gave me love and care.
Savannah Tarpley, Age 9

The Boys & Girls Club gave me a place to stay and to play. The Club gave me free trips to Sports*COM, the skating rink, and to bowling. It's a place to stay after school and do my homework too.
Jake Tarpley, Age 10

The Boys & Girls Club gave me a shirt and three cards. They gave me two hats and snacks.
Travis Stanley, Age 8

I like giving to other people, like people that don't have toys. I think giving is a good thing because giving is showing love to one another. Ms. Connie is my friend, and when I'm not with her, I miss her. She gives me love, and I give her love back. Love is good. Love is a gift that everybody can give. It's free to give also!
Shaquan Sneed, Age 6

The first day of school is always full of excitement. A new place, clothes, friends, and teachers all make up that first day. For the Boys & Girls Club, the first day for a new school year is exciting too. The summer has ended and the halls and rooms at the Club are full of chatter.

The greatest joy of giving came yesterday at the Club. A local sorority and their leader came by the Club to drop off school supplies for the children. You could hear the excitement ring throughout the Club. You just wouldn't believe the book bags, paper, pencils, crayons, scissors and so much more. The smiles from the children's faces lit up the whole room because no one knew that this would be the day that a group of people reached down in their pockets to spend their money and to give to the children. The Boys & Girls Club felt happy because they received something new for school.

Giving is more than reaching into your pockets. You must reach into the heart and give when there is nothing to give. If you

do this, you will be blessed threefold. This is what the sorority did that day. The Club wants to say "thank you" for giving us your donations and so much more. So, the next time you reach into your heart, please don't forget about the children at the Boys & Girls Club.
Connie Smith (Ms. Connie), Education Director

The Boys & Girls Club gave me my soul and spirit. Now I am a Christian.
Taylor Rutland, Age 8

The Boys & Girls Club has given me a place to stay after school. The Club gave me a place to play basketball with my friends. I am proud they gave me a place where people care about me and I can care about them.
Drew Woodard, Age 8

One day Mr. John gave me a snack, and it was my favorite. It was a chocolate chip cookie, and then I said thank you. Then I started helping him when I was done.
Stevie Moore, Age 9

The Boys & Girls Club has given me a place to play and have fun while my mom works. They gave me a place to make more friends.
Megan Sinvichith, Age 9

You should give by loving, supporting, and just by being there. You will find out that they really care. The Boys & Girls Club gives to everyone, not just the kids. So if everyone gives we can really make a difference.
Amanda Simons, Age 11

Giving is...

I give my love to my teacher and to the Boys & Girls Club. I think that if you give your time and support, you will love it. I help by passing out papers.
Jessica Simons, Age 8

I like to give to my friends, family and others. I share with others, and I like to give to the poor. I like my Boys & Girls Club.
Cody Bragg, Age 9

The Club gives us pool sticks and pool tables. They give us chairs to sit on and tables to do homework on. They gave us a place to go when our parents are not home. They gave me stuff to play with. I should thank them a lot. Thank you, Club.
Arianna Scott, Age 10

They Boys & Girls Club has given me a lot, like love and how to get along with other people. I love Ms. Emily and all the group leaders. Thank you a lot.
Jessica Simons, Age 8

I think that giving is something nice that people do because they want to. Like the staff at the Boys & Girls Club. They do a lot for the Club. And thanks to them, I have a place to play after school to meet new people. I am really thankful.
Hillary Garrett, Age 9

Chapter Three
One-Liners

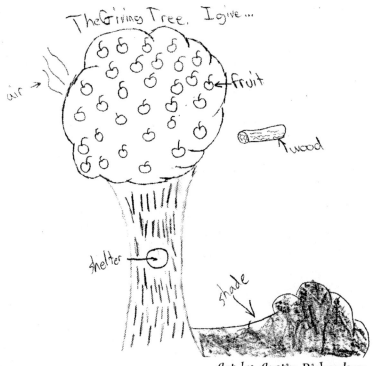

Art by Austin Richardson

If you give you might get a prize.
Kayla Walker, Age 9

My big brother gave me a ring because he loves me. His name is
Alex.
Danielle Walden, Age 7

I give my friends attention because they're nice.
Alex Atkins, Age 8

Giving is...

I love my sister and I give her presents.
Bobby Malone, Age 7

I give God love because I want to make God feel good.
Morgan Yandels, Age 7

I give God love because I love God and Jesus. I give God glory because He gives me life.
Bobby Malone, Age 7

I give people love because they love me back. God gave me love and I love God back.
Adam Ross, 5

I give my Mom hugs because I love her.
Itai Mapanga, Age 7

God gave us life. God gave us our world.
Morgan Yandels, Age 7

My Mom gave me a drink even though I was being bad, because she loves me.
Alex Atkins, Age 8

My Mom gives me money for no reason.
Katelyn Irving, Age 8

It is better to give than to receive.
DeKendra Lewis, Age 12

God gave us life.
Antoinette Jenkins, Age 8

God died to give us life with Him.
Jenna Ladd, Age 13

Our early ancestors gave us peace and independence.
Daniel Bernard, Age 13

God gave His love. God gave up Himself.
Jenna Ladd, Age 13

God gave Jesus to die for our sins.
Keenan Lewis, Age 8

God gave us faith, hope and joy.
DeKendra Lewis, Age 12

God gave us the Bible and the church.
Keenan Lewis, Age 8

God gave us friends and family to tell our problems to.
Jenna Ladd, Age 13

My brother gave me a Butterfinger, and the first thing I did was to give him a piece.
Allen Joiner, Age 10

My brother gave me a Playstation because he loves me.
Dillon Sweeney, Age 10

A girl in my neighborhood gave me friendship.
Morgan Yandels, Age 7

31

Giving is...

My God gave me life, and my parents gave me a Jevon Kearse jersey.
Ashley Malone, Age 11

My brother gave me a ring because he loves me.
Danielle Walden, Age 7

My sister gave me some paper, and I was happy because I could draw.
Dillon Melton, Age 8

I give love to my family.
Josh Hughey, Age 11

I give knowledge helping other people at school.
Michael Bianco, Age 11

I give love.
Alex Walden, Age 10

I give respect to elders.
Dillon Sweeney, Age 10

I give 10% of a lot of things to God.
Josh Hughey, Age 11

I give niceness.
Jessica Irwin, Age 9

I give effort, strength and time to play football.
Matt Weaver, Age 9

I give help when people need it. I helped someone at football practice on their homework.
John Weaver, Age 9

I give Santa cookies and milk once a year.
Matt Weaver, Age 9

In my old school I gave somebody some money to buy lunch.
Tony Roper, Age 9

I give time to help my little brother take a bath.
Forrest Roper, Age 8

I gave my girlfriend a kiss. I helped my grandmom mow the yard, and I helped my other grandmom mow her yard and then clean her room.
Alex Walden, Age 10

At the end of a Titans game, a little boy lost his Eddie George football because his friend kicked it, so I gave him mine. My dad got me another one.
John Weaver, Age 9

God gave us food to nurture our bodies to not go hungry.
DeKendra Lewis, Age 12

God gave us our personalities.
Jenna Ladd, Age 13

33

God gave us trees to have fresh air to breathe.
DeKendra Lewis, Age 12

Giving is...

If you give to a friend that is sad, it brightens someone's day.
DeKendra Lewis, Age 12

God gave us everything we need.
Breana Roberts, Age 6

God gave us the circle of life.
Daniel Bernard, Age 13

I gave my Nana a teddy bear so she wouldn't feel sad after she had back surgery.
Kaylan Cabrera, Age 6

My uncle gave me a watch so I can keep up with the time.
Marquise Lawrence, Age 10

My Nana gave me a dollar and it felt good.
Brooklyn Goolesby, 5

We probably wouldn't have anything if no one gave.
Aaron Parris, Age 11

Jesus gave His life on the cross for you, so give your life to Him.
Calvin French, Age 10

Giving is responsible sharing.
Deionte Edmonson, Age 6

I like giving. It is fun. I like it.
Brooke Duke, Age 9

The principal gave me a pencil in the cafeteria.
Stephen Duke, Age 7

I love to give.
Samantha Davis, Age 12

I helped my friend when he first came to the Club.
Jeff Davis, Age 9

I give to my dog, my cat and my bird.
Brandon Davis, Age 7

I love to give to my dad.
Justin Currey, Age 11

I gave apples to my friend.
Lakosha Cox, Age 11

When I gave somebody something it made me very proud.
Ben Cabrera, Age 10

I like to give to my brother and my mom and dad.
Chris Bush, Age 12

My mom gives me clothes and food and love.
Devon Brown, Age 9

Giving is important because it makes people happy.
Murphy Brazzell, Age 8

Giving is...

Giving is a fact of life.
Kacey Blackburn, Age 10

Jesus is the ultimate gift.
Michael Bianco, Age 11

God gave us food, house, trees, cars.
Demetrius Alford, Age 8

I give money to people. Somebody gave to me. I gave cans of food to the poor.
Antonio Adkerson, Age 9

Giving is so popular, the whole world depends on it.
Melissa Lee, Age 13

Giving makes me feel happy.
Teosha Lawrence, Age 7

God gave us His son.
Jenna Ladd, Age 13

God gives us food.
Kalesha Johnson, Age 7

I love to give. Giving is living.
Alex Johnson, Age 14

Giving is...ice cream.
Sarah Jarrett, Age 8

Giving is nice and very good.
Christine Jarrett, Age 11

Giving is love and fun from everywhere to me to you.
Halee Gregory, Age 9

Giving is good, just like how the clouds give us rain, snow, hail and life.
Kyle Goolesby, Age 11

Spiders give us help by eating insects.
Kacey Blackburn, Age 10

Always give someone something.
Ben Cabrera, Age 10

God gave us the earth and life. The earth gave us food too.
Brandon Davis, Age 8

Cows give us milk.
Hillary Garrett, Age 9

Trees and plants give us oxygen.
Kacey Blackburn, Age 10

I gave my mother flowers from Kmart. My poppa gave me the money.
Alex Garner, Age 6

37
....

When giving, I feel important.
Adrian Rippy, Age 13

Giving is...

Giving to the world is what God did. You should give to people.
Keywannia Pickett, Age 13

Ladybugs give me good luck.
Randi Moore, Age 10

God gave us light to see in the dark.
Kacey Blackburn, Age 10

I love to give flowers.
Hillary Garrett, Age 9

My teacher gave me a good grade.
Randi Moore, Age 10

Giving is where you give something to someone with no intention of receiving.
Michael Moore, Age 11

I like giving poor people presents.
Kacey Blackburn, Age 10

Giving is the best thing to do for a friend that you like very much.
Clinton McClendon, 16

Once somebody gave me a dollar and I felt happy.
Cody Martin, Age 7

My mom makes me feel safe with hugs. My mom loves me.
Marissa Williams, Age 7

My cousin is giving me a cat.
Tyler Whiteman, Age 9

Giving means a lot to me.
Ben Cabrera, Age 10

I like to give to my brother and sister.
Travis Whiteman, Age 11

I like to give clothes to the foster kids, and I give food to the poor.
Nick Warren, Age 11

The one who gives gets a hand.
Kayla Walker, Age 9

Sometimes people give us what we want.
Kacey Blackburn, Age 10

I gave my friend a game because he did not have one.
Justin Walker, Age 10

Giving is helping.
Leeah Turner, Age 6

Giving is when the flowers bloom.
Savannah Tarpley, Age 9

Giving is fun, just like sharing, so give to a friend and share with them.
Nick Warren, Age 11

Giving is...

There is one thing some people do not know how to do. It's to give and be good and love.
Kayla Walker, Age 9

Mr. John gives us a snack after school.
Kacey Blackburn, Age 10

Giving is believing.
Halee Gregory, Age 9

Chapter Four
Family

I Love To Give My Family

Art by Ashley Woodard

One day someone did not have any lunch or snack so I gave them some of my candy bar. It feels good because I did something nice for someone.
Aaron Parris, Age 11

Once two of my friends didn't have a pencil, so I gave them both one. I felt happy because I did something nice.
Tashinga Mapanga, Age 10

Giving is...

One day I needed help with something and my friend helped me. I felt good and I was happy.
Maylan Yandels, Age 11

One day I went to the mall. My grandmother was with me, and she bought me an outfit and a new shirt. I told her thank you and that I love her.
Brittany Wherry, Age 11

One day I let Mr. Daniel use a pen. I felt happy.
Aaron Parris, Age 11

Once a friend had no snack and I gave her a muffin and she was glad.
Tashinga Mapanga, Age 11

One day my step-dad gave me speed skates for my birthday, and they had to have been worth $200. I told him I loved him a lot.
Brittany Wherry, Age 11

Here is what I did for my mom: I helped her move into our new house. I helped the most because I was looking forward to it. I almost asked my mom if she would pay me, but then I decided I would rather not because she shouldn't have to pay me to help her.
Arianna Scott, Age 10

I'm giving a present to my dad on his birthday. It makes me feel good. It makes him feel good, too. That way, everybody is happy.
Justin White, Age 13

My mother gave me birth, and I give my mother love. My dad gave me a place to live. God gave birth to my mother and everybody else. I give my love to God.
Matt Weaver, Age 9

How do I feel when I give? How do you feel when you give? Questions like these pop up in our minds from time to time. Giving makes me feel good inside, knowing I'm helping someone less fortunate than me.
Lauren Walker, Age 12

My mom gives me love. My dad gives me love, too. My family gives me love.
Kayla Walker, Age 9

I love my mom and dad. They give me things. I gave my friend a "best friend" ring. My family gives me stuff, and my friend gave me a "best friend" necklace. My grandfather gave me a ring. I gave a bear to my mom. I gave a cup to my dad. I gave a new toy to my cousin. My aunt took me to the store and bought me earrings. I gave all of my little clothes to the children who need them. My mom bought a necklace for me.
Bethanie Wallace, Age 9

I love to give. I love to see the face of a person when I give them something. I think everyone should give something to someone. My cousins are very cute when I give them something.
Nikki Trice, Age 13

It is good to give food, toys and clothes to poor people. Money too. I felt a lot better when I did it.
Alicia Todd, Age 8

I have shared my pencil with my friend. I gave someone a piece of paper. I gave a present to my friend.
Jake Tarpley, Age 10

Giving is...

Giving is a very important thing in this world. I wish that everyone in the world would give to someone. Inside of me, I feel that even if someone picks on you and bothers you, they may still care for you just the tiniest bit. Giving to me doesn't only mean giving to a person.

A different way you can give to someone is to give to nature and maybe pick up trash or plant trees in the park. Giving can mean a lot of different things to different people.

In my heart giving is one of the most important things. If people didn't give to others, a lot of people may not have what they have today. We are all very fortunate to have what we have, and I think that a lot of us take things for granted. Maybe we should all just sit and think a while about people in different countries and think what we would do if we were them. If we all thought that we were that way, maybe a lot of people would give people like that a lot more stuff and not talk about them all of the time. We all don't know what they go through, so it's like that old saying, "Don't judge a book by it's cover."

Well, let's all just think, and maybe you will start giving a little more and start caring about people.
Jessica Walls, Age 13

When I gave my friend a stuffed animal, I felt good. Then she gave me a purple purse, and that made me feel good. It made her feel good too. We were really good friends. That's what giving means.
Savannah Tarpley, Age 9

My friends are Kyle, Bruce and CJ. They help me with my work at school. After school they help me with homework. Kyle helps me with math, CJ helps me with science, and Bruce helps me with handwriting. They are very nice to help me with my stuff.
Travis Stanley, Age 8

Giving is like helping old people across the road and helping them cut their yard.
Austin Mersinger, Age 10

Today my friend's brother is dead. He died because he got sick. He got so sick that he died. Amber cried for days. I feel so sad because he was my best friend too. He was my friend since I was a baby. I wish I could see him. I miss him. I can't give him anything anymore.
Samantha Spencer, Age 14

I gave my friend a toy before and he liked it. He really liked it and he gave me something. But one day he gave it back to me and I said, "Why are you giving it back to me?" He wanted me to have it.
Anthony Smith, Age 10

Giving is like giving your love, time and support. I helped a boy that goes to my school. I helped him speak like me and write like me.
Jessica Simons, Age 8

I love giving because it makes people happy. It also makes people smile. Plus it makes me happy because they're happy.
Donann Melton, Age 11

One day I saw a little boy learning to ride his bike, so I helped him. Pretty soon he was riding his bike up and down the streets.
Adam McCormack, Age 10

I gave my old bike to my cousin and she was very happy when she got it, so I felt so happy. When she got it, my Mom cried a little. My cousin's name is Kim. She is my best cousin.
Nicole Maynard, Age 11

I gave my uncle a toy truck for his collection. I wanted him to have it so he could remember me when he went off to the Navy. I miss him.
Cody Maynard, Age 7

Giving is...

In cheerleading and gymnastics, you have to put in a lot of time and effort. When you do back handsprings and cheers, you have to be loud and strong. So, even though you might not realize it, you can give through sports. There are a lot of things you can give through. For example, teaching a dog to sit and trust me is very liberating. So, don't think that you can only give kindness. It doesn't stop there.
Amanda Manning, Age 13

Giving is when my brother shares with me, even though I know that he really doesn't want to. But that's just it...it's the thought that counts. Even though I don't like him very much sometimes, I still love him enough to give him anything he needs, even if he doesn't give back. I give him love, encouragement, support and advice. This makes me happy.
DeAndrea Mack, Age 12

The one who saw sadness gave. The one who didn't will regret it. Maybe for life.
Kayla Walker, Age 9

I helped my friend talk, walk, read and eat. She likes me now. She said thank you very much.
Brittany Zygadlo, Age 8

I gave God love and He gave me love. God gave us food and shelter. But the biggest thing of all He gave us is life.

I gave my friend Gooze and he gave me Pokémon cards. They are really special to me.

We live with my grandmother and she helps us a lot. She opened her house to me and my mom and sister. She loves us very much.

Morgan Yandels, Age 7

Giving makes me feel good. When giving, I feel happy. I love to give because it's nice. I love to share my bat. I love to give birthday presents.
Drew Woods, Age 7

This is what I think giving is: I think giving is when you give something to someone, and it doesn't matter who. This is what I do. I give to the needy and my dogs and cat. I give food to the needy. I give clothes. I give clothes to my family that are too small for me.
Jessica Williams, Age 11

I gave someone clothes, toys and food. Someone gave me a pair of shoes. I gave my mom a flower. My dad gave me a Bears hat. I gave my dad a baseball.
Jordan Wood, Age 8

When I give something, it makes me feel good that I give food or clothes. Or if I help someone, it makes me feel good inside. Teaching people something that they might learn, know forever, then teach it to someone else makes me feel good inside. I feel good inside when I give food to people so they don't go hungry, and I feel good about myself when I gave them clothes to keep them warm for the winter. That is what I feel about giving.
Lindsey Davenport, Age 11

It makes me feel good to give. Sometimes I will carry something for somebody, and that's giving. I gave my mom a present. Being a mom, she was happy that I gave it to her. I gave my friend something just to be nice. He is nice to me. I have fun with him.
James Williams, Age 9

I would give something of mine but I don't really have a lot to give. If some of my friends needed it though, I would give it anyway. I give to my brother, sister, mom and dad.
Travis Whiteman, Age 11

Giving is...

I gave my brother a backpack, a bike and tennis shoes. I gave my family love and care. I gave my sister a baseball, bike and care. I gave the Boys & Girls Club love, care and kindness.

My grandpa gave me a BB gun, a bike, an alarm clock and his friendship. I gave my mom a bird, a dress and shoes. I gave my dad a tie, a shirt and a watch.
Tyler Whiteman, Age 9

My mom and dad are nice to me. My brothers are nice to me. My gramma and grandpa are nice to me. My Aunt Kim is nice to me too. My cat is nice, she comes to give me hugs.
Jessica Whiteman, Age 8

I give presents of money to friends on their birthdays. It makes me feel good to see them smile.
Justin White, Age 13

One day, my friend Alex asked me if I wanted to ride bikes with him. I said yes, and I let him use my bike. He asked me, "Can I have your bike?" I said yes. Then he rode it home. I felt good.
Stevie Moore, Age 9

Someone gave me a jacket. I gave someone clothes, food and toys. Giving is more important because you are being very nice and thankful.
Jordan Wood, Age 8

My mom and dad give me love because I am their child. My sisters give me love because I give them love. My brothers give me love because I give them love. My whole big family gives me love, and I love them so, so much.
Randi Moore, Age 10

I give to my friends and family. When I give to people, it makes me feel good.
Michael Moore, Age 11

I gave some toys to the Day Care because I didn't want them anymore. I felt good about that because I like to share. Giving is good. I like to share. It is fun because when I share, I don't always have to get something back unless they give something back. When I give, I'm real excited, because if you share, it tells them that you want to be their friend.
Savannah Tarpley, Age 9

I will share with others. I will take care of others. I will play with someone who doesn't have a friend. I will play and share all the time. Giving is sharing with one another. I will care for others. I will talk with others. I will love others.
Britney Moore, Age 8

By giving to someone and not receiving anything, you know what giving is about. If you received after giving every time, you would not be giving.

Giving has always been something I have been used to. Because my mother gave me life, I am willing to give myself to anyone in need.

Through giving, you can learn a lot of different things. Memories are giving because the people you share them with will always remember the time you shared with them.
Emil Mitchell (Mr. Emil), Staff

I think giving is a good thing because my mom gives me a whole lot of money every morning for school. They said if you give, you get more than you gave, so you should always give because something good will come out of it.
Liqa Minter, Age 12

Giving makes me feel good. Giving is to give money to the poor. I think people should give every day.
Michael Moore, Age 11

Giving is...

One time I gave money to my church. I gave food to my brother. Sometimes I give my mom a present. I give toys away to friends. My mom gave me a dog for my birthday.
Dylan Perry, Age 10

You should give because God our Father gave His life to us. He died on the cross for our sins. Since He gave something to us, we should give love, happiness, and peace back to Him. We shouldn't only give to God, but we should also give to other people. Giving is a great thing to do.
Keywannia Pickett, Age 13

I love to give people stuff. I like to help. When I give people stuff it makes me happy.

People have given me stuff. I've given them stuff. Give food to the poor people.

People giving you stuff is nice. You giving people stuff is nice. Everything about giving is nice.
Cassandra Peppers, Age 9

I give people back what belongs to them. It makes me feel like I am happy about doing what's right. The Lord wants me to know what's right from wrong. When praises go up, blessings come down.
Mike Oden, Age 13

My mom gave me some money for my birthday, and I gave my mom some flowers. She gave me a treat, and when it was her birthday, I gave her a vase to put her flowers in. She gave me ten dollars and bought a rose.
Tra Norwood, Age 7

When my classmates do not know how to work problems in math, science, social studies, reading or spelling, I help them.
Eric Hughes, Age 9

I gave my baseball cards to my friend, and I felt happy because Michael asked me.

One day I went to my Nanny's house. She needed help cleaning her house. I was washing clothes and vacuuming the floor. I helped her make dinner.
Stevie Moore, Age 9

Here you go, mom. Here's a special gift just for you for Mother's Day. I hope you like it. See, to me giving is special because I really feel good inside.
Jasmine Haynes, Age 9

I give love and care to my family members. I especially give lots of love to my other great-grandmother. She is 92. I help her by fixing her meals and walking with her.
Halee Gregory, Age 9

Giving means to give someone something without getting something back. When I give something to someone, it makes me feel good because it's helping people get stuff done faster.

Giving means a lot to me because it feels good. If we didn't have giving, everybody wouldn't be helping people.
Kyle Goolesby, Age 11

Giving makes me feel good, and giving is something that you do for somebody. I like to give people stuff. I gave my mom a glass for Easter, and it made me and her feel good.
Jasmine Goolesby, Age 9

Giving is something that you do or give to show someone you care about them. One day I was sad, and my sister gave me a hug to cheer me up.
Hillary Garrett, Age 9

Giving is...

The old saying goes, "It's better to give than receive." I find this statement very true. When I give to someone, it makes me feel so happy. The look on someone's face makes you want to burst into laughter. I love to see someone after they get a big present. They're just so cheerful. I think I prefer giving over receiving.

God is a perfect example of a giving person. Not only did He give His only son Jesus Christ, but He gives us something to look forward to every day. He provides someone to talk to. He gives you so much, but a lot of people take Him for granted. Just keep in mind He loves you anyway.
Hali Garrett, Age 13

I help my mom do dishes. I helped my sister learn how to ride a bike. My brother taught me how to tie my shoes.
Jake Tarpley, Age 10

Giving is for Christians that believe in God and Jesus. It's good for our hearts and souls and spirits.
Taylor Rutland, Age 9

Giving can mean giving your time. I gave my little sister my time to help her with her homework and I love her. I love you, Boys & Girls Club.
Jessica Simons, Age 8

I would give my hair to a little girl and she would give me her life. I would give my hair to a person with cancer. I would go to the beauty parlor and they would cut my hair and I would give it to her. I love to give because it's nice. When giving, I feel good. Giving makes me feel good. I love to give, but I don't have to receive.
Brittany Zygadlo, Age 9

I like to give. I give to my mom and dad. I give to my brother and sister. I give to my family. I give to my friends.
Travis Whiteman, Age 11

Someone gave me a backpack. I gave someone food and toys and clothes. Giving is important because you are caring.
Jordan Wood, Age 8

Giving is when you let someone have something without getting something back. A person who gives without receiving is a nice and thoughtful person. I wish all people were like that.
DeAndrea Mack, Age 12

I gave my friend a skateboard, because he didn't have one, and he really liked skateboards.
Adam McCormack, Age 10

I give to the poor. It makes me feel good. I love to give things to people. I love to give on Christmas. I give presents and hugs. I like to give stuff to people. Giving always comes from your heart. I like giving food to the homeless. I hate to see people cry.
Austin Mersinger, Age 10

When I give, I feel like I am helping someone out. When I give, I give clothes that are too small, but very clean and very cute. I give to needy families. I give to my animals. I give can food to needy people. It makes me feel good because I feel like I am helping someone out. I just feel so great.
Jessica Williams, Age 11

I like to give some people things and it makes them happy. Sometimes people do not deserve it, but some people deserve it. But I give anyway.
Cassandra Peppers, Age 9

I give toys and clothes. I help my aunt clean her house. Giving is very fun. Giving is the best.
Michael Moore, Age 11

Giving is...

I love giving, but I really don't like receiving. I really hate receiving. I just like giving to poor people that don't have a cent. I would give my soul, heart and spirit to God and Jesus if I had to. I will do what God and Jesus and the Holy Spirit say.

I'm going to tell you a sad story about my pets. I had two horses, one cow, one cat, and a dog that had five puppies (three died). We sold the mom and one puppy. We kept one. He grew up and ran away. My cow died too. But I gave them all love and took care of them.
Taylor Rutland, Age 9

I like giving because it is something you should do. God gives, you give, and other people give. That gives you the reason to give to people and elderly. It makes me feel good when I give to people. When I help little kids, I feel good about helping. I feel very good about giving to people who don't have food or clothes. When they don't have food or clothes, that makes me feel sad because they need help. It makes me feel like I need to give them the things they need. I should give them love, respect and prayers.
Keywannia Pickett, Age 13

I gave my sister five dollars because she didn't have any money. She wanted a school Barbie and it cost nine dollars and she had four. So we added our money and it equaled nine.
Majlik Roach, Age 10

I gave a toy car. I gave a shell. I gave a doll. I gave some shoes. I gave ice cream.
Tia Roach, Age 8

If you give, you bring love to the hearts of others. I believe in giving and sharing and helping others. Giving makes me happy.
Adrian Rippy, Age 13

I give my time to walk my dog.
I give my time to share with all.
I give my time from within.
I love sharing with my friends.
Austin Richardson, Age 13

Giving is special because it is a nice thing to do. I like it because I gave a friend one of my toys and it was a nice and very cool thing to do. It was my idea, and I am a nice person.
Asa Proctor, Age 8

One time this kid had damage to his brain and I helped him learn stuff.

I feel very happy when I give to people. It makes me feel very good.

I like to help people because it makes me feel free.
Stephen Price, Age 10

I am thankful to be born. I'm thankful to have a nice family, and for my clothes, my bed to sleep in, and my backpack to put my books in for school. I'm thankful for my school, my sister, my teacher, my doctor, my friends. I am thankful for the people who help me with homework. I'm thankful to be adopted, for my pets, my home, for food, to be at the Boys & Girls Club, and how they help me. I like to give to my sister, friends, teachers, doctors, and my pets. I like to help people do the right thing, to make the right choice. I like to help my friends not to take drugs. I had a best friend and she died because she got in the car with people who took drugs and they got in in a wreck. She was only 13. I wish that she was still here, but she made the wrong choice. If she had made the right choice, she would be alive right now. I think of her every day. It makes me sad just to think about it. I would give her everything if she were still here.
Samantha Spencer, Age 14

Giving is...

Giving makes me feel happy sometimes. I might give my favorite toy. It is real fun. Giving sometimes makes me feel great because I know I help poor people. It makes me feel like a Christian. Giving makes me feel good. It is real nice to give stuff because people are real poor. It is kind of sad.
Taylor Rutland, Age 9

The principals are very giving people. The real principal is a very giving person. He gives us pencils in the cafeteria. He is very nice.
Stephen Duke, Age 7

One time my great-grandpa was hurt and very sick and I helped him fix some breakfast. I also helped him walk outside and look at pretty birds.

One time my dog was hurt. I went to tell my mom and she cured my dog to health.
Stephen Price, Age 10

Giving to people in need makes me feel good about myself. I feel that, if I was in need, I'd want people to help me through my times of need. Giving to people is sharing, and sharing is caring. I try my best to help people that are in need so that maybe they'll help the next person that comes along in their life.

I like helping younger children so that, when they get older, they'll help someone else during life. People could be giving by helping someone with their homework. Also people can give by just letting people talk to you so they can get stuff off their chest.

Giving is an important thing in life, so everyone should do it.
Jessica Walls, Age 13

There was a boy who was in a car wreck. He lost his parents and was paralyzed. I pushed him around and helped him go places he couldn't.

There was a girl who came from Russia who didn't speak our language. I helped her speak and write English words.
Jacob Price, Age 10

I give love to my mom and dad. I help my mom clean the house. I help my dad clean the yard.
Bryon Price, Age 10

Giving is fun because it's what Christians do. It helps people that are poor. It will help them get the needed shelter, water, food and clothes.
Taylor Rutland, Age 9

My step mom is nice to me. Ms Hall is nice to me. Mr. John is nice to me. My dad is nice to me. My sisters are nice to me. My brothers are nice to me. My best friend is nice to me. Mr. Steve is nice to me. My teacher is nice to me. They all give me love.
Austin Poteete, Age 8

Giving is something you do or even say that's from the heart. I'm in cheerleading, and I cheer for my team and my school. I love doing it because I like to cheer and give my teammates and the football players all the support they could need and have. That's what I do and that's how I give.
Olivia Preston, Age 12

My best friend gave me a ring. I have helped a little girl. I have been able to go to a nursing home with our Girl Scout troop and give the people flowers.
Amanda Pierce, Age 9

One day I gave my third grade teacher a candle. She felt good and I felt good too. She was taking me to school to let me help her. She called her daughter and told her to get me chicken nuggets. I felt good when she got me food to take care of me.
Jasmine Goolesby, Age 9

Giving is...

I gave Samantha two of my horses and a picture of me that she put in her photo album.
Sareda Calderon, Age 12

Giving makes me feel very, very good and proud. You should always feel good. Giving is the main idea you should be proud of the most. Give from the heart. Giving always comes from your heart when you are being kind enough to give somebody else something.
Ben Cabrera, Age 10

I like to give to the earth, my church, people, my brother, my mom and my dad.
Chris Bush, Age 12

I love giving because it is a nice thing to do. Giving makes me feel so good. My heart feels so good when I give somebody a new toy.
Randi Moore, Age 10

I can give my Gameboy to someone or my Nintendo 64 to someone. I will give my whole room away. I will give my food away. I will give my whole house away. I will give my car away.

I gave away a lot of stuff and haven't gotten anything back.

Giving is to give someone something and not receiving anything back. If you give and get something back, that's not really giving.
Kyle Goolesby, Age 11

I like to give out a pair of shoes, and I like to give out clothes.
Travis Whiteman, Age 11

I gave my mom something for Valentine's Day. She was happy.
James Williams, Age 9

I give toys and games to the Goodwill for the kids who have no stuff. It makes me feel good.

I like to give to the people who do not have any games or toys. I give food to my brother too.
Chris Bush, Age 12

My brother gives me Pokémon cards and he protects me. His name is Joshua. He helps me with my homework. He feeds me sometimes, too.

My grandmother gives me sweets. She gives me food and she gives me love. She gave me a scooter and she takes me to the greenway.

The store gives me food. My mom gives me shoes. My teachers give me laughter. My dad gives me love. My mom gives me a ride to school.
Devon Brown, Age 9

Giving makes me feel good. When I give, I feel happy. I love to give because it feels nice. When giving to other people, I feel proud.

I love to give people things they need. I give my brother stuff. I love giving stuff to other people. I love to give, and they don't have to pay me back. I help people with their homework.
Anastasia Brobst, Age 9

My friend gave me a Cardinals hat and I gave him a nerf gun for his birthday. He gave me a baseball card. I was glad that he gave me a baseball card.

Giving is important. When you give, you are happy. When you give something to someone, it lets them know you care about them. And if they give you something cool to play with, that's fun too.
Murphy Brazzell, Age 8

Giving is special because I like it. It is free and you share it with friends.
Ashtyn Baty, Age 8

Giving is...

I give to the poor and my friends give me stuff too. I like my friends and family. My friend gives me toys. God gave me hands to hold stuff.

One day I found a dog, and I kept it at my house and fed it. I helped my mom and dad hang pictures.

I wash the car for people. My friend came to my house. He was hot, just like me, so I gave him some shoes and then gave some people a desk. I help my mom's boyfriend by doing yard work. I like to help others. I help my dad work on cars and stuff.
Cody Bragg, Age 9

One of the things I give the most is advice. Not just school advice, or writing advice, but I give advice on things from drawing to social advice. I like to help people out a lot. Most of the time people take my advice. One thing about my advice is that it's in depth. I think about it a lot and it works most of the time. Every time I see a problem, I can solve it. Most of the time, that is. So, most of the time advice is my best gift.
Michael Bianco, Age 11

There once was a cat named June. He caught a mouse and gave it to his friend BoBo. They are best friends.
Alexis Atkins, Age 8

Giving is a wonderful thing. Everybody can give if it's your birthday or if it's Christmas. Some gifts don't come in packages or boxes, and don't have shapes or sizes. I give gifts like that every day. I give my mom hugs before school. I give her a kiss after school. I give her a hug and kiss just because when I want to. I give her love and care when she needs it, or even if she doesn't. Instead of a wrapped up gift, I give love. I give clothes to the outreach center and to my little sister. I have two sisters, and I give love and gifts. So there are two types of gifts, maybe even a bunch more.
Chelsee Barbo, Age 13

We should give people food and presents and other things like clothes and a home. I can give to my mom and dad and my grandma. It makes me feel like I should be the one that needs food and clothes.
Charles Arms, Age 11

I took time off from doing my homework to help the preschool kids at my Bible class. I help my brother with his math and science.
Anthony Alston, Age 10

Giving is something everyone does at some point in time. For instance, it is what parents do day in and day out. Parents give their love and they care for us. Also, they put food and drinks on the table for us. They give us gifts for Christmas and sometimes we don't even say thank you. Sometimes we take our parents for granted, like they're supposed to do the things they do for us. I love my parents. I realize that I need to give them something. I need to show them my respect and love.
Chaisson Allen, Age 12

I gave three dollars to a boy that was crying and he stopped crying. It made me happy.
William Akins, Age 8

Murfreesboro gave me a church where I go every Wednesday and Sunday until noon to worship my Father.
Briana Luchtefeld, Age 13

One time I gave my best friend a puppy. I was so happy. One day later the puppy died and I was sad. Then I told him he could have another one. He got one, and I was happy again.
Sam Loyd, Age 8

Giving is...

I got a dog from my dad. The only thing wrong was that she had the mange. That's an illness that makes her hair fall out. The other dogs got it and died. But I still had her. Then when she was two years old, she ran away. But a year later, I got a two-year-old dog named Reba. I love her a lot. I still miss my other dog, but at least I have one.
Katie Lower, Age 11

My brother gave me a bear because we were helping each other clean the house. It made me feel good. When someone is sad, you should give them your heart, or a puppy.
Teosha Lawrence, Age 7

To me, giving is a good thing to do because some people are homeless. Giving makes me feel happy because other people don't have stuff like we do.
I like giving my old stuff away so I can have enough room for my new stuff. I like giving my old stuff away so that other kids can have some more stuff to play with.
Marquise Lawrence, Age 9

My family is from Mexico. We give each other food, clothes, and love. I like helping people. We help each other.
Sareda Calderon, Age 11

I give people toys, clothes, and games. God gave me hands to hold stuff, feet to walk with, eyes to see stuff, and a brain and mind to think with.
Christian Johnson, Age 9

There was a Chinese girl that came from China, and I taught her how to speak our language.
Bryon Price, Age 10

I gave my attention and my respect and care to kids and adults that could not talk or hear or see.
Michael Moore, Age 11

I gave a rose and teddy bear and a backpack. I gave five dollars and she really likes it. I'll give my heart and soul for my dog because she is so good to me.
Majlik Roach, Age 10

Giving is so lovely. Giving is very important to me. It makes me and others feel good. When I give, it makes me feel I have done something special.
Adrian Rippy, Age 13

Giving makes me feel so much better. It makes you feel good to know that you're touching someone by doing just little things like giving your time or even just giving your clothes to other people that can't afford it. It makes the other people feel special and liked. When you give to someone, it just makes them so happy. The look on their face when they've received a gift from you – it just makes you feel so glad. Giving is a special, precious thing. Try to give as much as you can. I'm sure you'll find it makes you feel a lot better.
Hali Garrett, Age 13

Yesterday was my birthday and my friends gave me some presents. I felt good and so did they. I invited them to my party at the bowling alley.
Jasmine Goolesby, Age 9

A man gave a radio to a young boy. Giving is to give someone something and love them too. Giving is a special gift.
Kyle Goolesby, Age 11

I gave some flowers. I gave love. I gave a hat. I gave a shirt. I gave a toy.
Tia Roach, Age 8

63

Giving is...

Once I gave somebody something because they needed it more than me. It felt good.
Ben Cabrera, Age 10

Reading books is great for me. Books are about stories, learning and rules of history. The experience of life can be found in fiction and non-fiction books. A library is a place that has a collection of books, pamphlets and reference books.
Mike Oden, Age 13

Giving is fun. Giving is what God wants us to do. If you give, you'll feel good inside about going to heaven. I give to my family.
Christian Johnson, Age 9

Giving is something you give to someone else. A lot of people give canned food to people that don't have food or money. My grandfather gives food to people that don't have any food. He goes to the cafeteria and gets warm food and gives it to the people.
Halee Gregory, Age 9

Giving is a good thing to do. Everybody should give willingly, which means to do it even if you don't want to. I always give to people all the time, but sometimes I don't want to. I give to my family, friends and strangers. I haven't met anyone who is poor except a couple people. I would give to them too.
Brittany Johnson, Age 11

I give to my little sister. It makes me feel good knowing I helped someone. I feel generous that I'm giving to someone that can't do all the things I do. How would you feel if there was someone who was less fortunate and had no food? Wouldn't you feed them? I would because I would feel bad knowing I could help someone. That's what giving means to me.
Ashley Johnson, Age 12

One Christmas my friend got me an Easy Bake oven. I like giving a lot and I also like people giving me things too. I don't like it when people are mean to me. I like it when I go to art because they give me paper to draw on.
Sarah Jarrett, Age 8

When I went to my grandmother's house she gave me twenty dollars. I gave my friend a watch for his birthday.
Tra Norwood, Age 7

I help handicapped people every year. I give toys and clothes to people that don't have any good clothes.

When my mom had a bad car accident, she broke her leg and her spinal cord. I helped her a lot. I helped her do chores.

My friend helps me with homework. I love giving to people because it is nice. When giving, I feel proud. I love to give but don't have to receive. Giving makes me feel very good. Giving is very, very nice to do to people.
Anastasia Brobst, Age 9

My mom is nice to me. My sister is not that nice to me. My brother is nice to me a lot, but not as much as my mom. I would give her anything.
Sarah Jarrett, Age 8

One day I gave a kid 25 cents for snack. He said he was going to give me a quarter back. I felt good that I helped him get a snack.

I helped my great-grandpa around the house and raked the yard.
Zach Jackson, Age 9

My mom gave me a backpack and my dad gave me two dogs. I gave my mom a cap. God gave me my mom and my two dads.
Keenen Jackson, Age 7

Giving is...

Giving is a nice thing to do. I like giving people things. It makes people happy, and me happy too.
Theodoria Ingram, Age 7

Giving is to use your own spare time to help others with housework and other things like that. I help by vacuuming.
Eric Hughes, Age 9

When I give to my sister, it makes me feel happy. I will give to most anybody that needs it. I am not a very nice person, but I give to some people. When I give, I feel very happy.
Cameron Fye, Age 11

One day a new boy came to school. He didn't know anyone. So I showed him around school, and he made some new friends.
Adam McCormack, Age 10

I gave my mom a get-well card. It said, "Hope you get better soon." I gave it to her because I love her.
Austin Mersinger, Age 10

I will play with others. I will help others. I will take care of others. Giving is sharing with others. I will care for others. I will talk with others. I will love others. I will play with someone who doesn't have a friend.
Brooke Fye, Age 5

I like giving because it's nice and it's cool. I like giving and being nice. I like giving because it's kind.
Giving is polite. Once I gave somebody my notebook because I had an extra one. One time I gave a man something to drink. He didn't have anything.
Michael Fults, Age 10

Giving is a good thing, especially if you give to poor people. They will really like it. Even if you are giving to your parents, they will really like it.
Derrick Ferguson, Age 13

My granny helps me keep up my room. She makes me spaghetti and meatballs. They are delicious. They are the best in the whole world.

I have to go now and play baseball with Mr. Steve. He is so nice and he wears glasses. He gives us kids love.

My teacher is so nice and young. She giggles and makes me laugh too.
Kayla Dyer, 5

My cousin gave me a snake. I gave my cousin an iguana. Giving made me feel happy. I like receiving gifts, but I enjoy giving them more.
Bruce Dunkerson, Age 8

I like giving. It's fun. You can give flowers to people. You can give people lots of stuff. I give people cards and presents too. It is good to give. It makes them happy and surprised. I went with my Girl Scout troop to the hospital and colored pictures and gave them away. We planted flowers too. I like giving because it makes people happy.
Brooke Duke, Age 9

A lot of times people are nice to me and I think that is very respectful. And in a way that is giving.
Briana Luchtefeld, Age 13

I am glad that God gave me life. I am glad He gave me talent. He gave me family who loves me and takes care of me.

I give my heart and soul to my friends. The reason why is because I love them and I am really close to my friends.
Chaisson Allen, Age 12

Giving is...

I have spent time with my sisters and taught them how to play games and ride bikes. Giving should mean a lot to everybody, like it does to me.
Ben Cabrera, Age 10

Giving is important because a lot of people don't have a lot. One of my friends doesn't have a lot, so I gave her a coat and she didn't say thank you. She never even wore it. I was upset because I wanted to help her, but she didn't like it. I told my mom, and she said that the important thing was that I wanted to help her. She said that I did my part.
Katie Lower, Age 11

Giving is good. Giving is great. Giving is God's creation. When I give something to someone, it makes me feel happy and proud. I love giving from the heart. When I give, it makes me feel a certain way. I love giving every day.
Once I gave a hundred dollars to charity. The name of the charity was Goodwill, and I gave to help them out.
Jordan Davis, Age 10

I helped my friend. He had a wreck on his bike. He did not wear his helmet. He hurt his head. I helped him get to the house.
Jeff Davis, Age 9

One time I had a friend who didn't have the money for a t-shirt. So, I went home and thought about it and decided to buy one for him. I went to the place where the t-shirt was, bought it for him, gave it to him. That was an act of giving.
Michael Moore, Age 11

My brother gave me a computer game. Since he gave me a game, I gave him a new clock. He loves his new clock. He uses it all the time.
Taylor Rutland, Age 8

I like giving something to someone because it feels good. I like it because I am appreciated when I give. When I give something to someone or tutor someone, I feel good because everything works out good. That's why I feel good about giving something.

When I was seven years old, I didn't like to give. When it was my birthday, I brought cupcakes to class. I didn't want to share my cupcakes, but my mom said I had to give them to everybody. Then I started to cry. My mom said I could have two cupcakes, then I stopped crying. I was beginning to learn what giving is about.
Kyle Goolesby, Age 11

My sisters give me love all the time. I hope that when they get old enough to come to the Club, they can. I think the staff can teach them about life.
Hillary Garrett, Age 9

My mom gives me stuff for my birthday and for Christmas. She gives me stuff when I get an A on my report card. I get toys when I make A's and B's. When I do well on my tests, I get toys from my mom.
Brandon Davis, Age 8

I gave my sister a present for her birthday. My mom gives me money. Cody gave me 75 cents. I gave Cody $1.50 and he gave me 50 cents. I gave my other friend a dollar. I gave my friends toys. I gave Robert some Pokémon cards.
Jeff Davis, Age 9

When I help someone, like giving food or clothing, that makes me feel very good inside. You can give by lending a hand, giving blood to help people, giving money to people and giving them warm, fresh food and clean clothes, nice and warm where they don't get wet.
Lindsey Davenport, Age 11
Christine Jarrett, Age 11

69

Giving is...

I give to my friends and I feel good. I give to my cousins and relatives and it feels good. I give to my Mom and Dad on Mother's Day and Father's Day. Giving is fun. I like to run to people and give.
Justin Currey, Age 11

I gave my snack to my cousin because he left his at home. I feel good about giving. He doesn't have to give me anything. I feel proud about myself.
Lakosha Cox, Age 11

I think giving is a great thing to do. I give people stuff because it's nice and fun. I think more people should give just like me.
Brittany Johnson, Age 11

Giving is a wonderful thing. Sometimes gifts are wrapped in pretty bows. Sometimes they're even wrapped in ugly bows or none at all. Or sometimes they're wrapped in love and care.
Chelsee Barbo, Age 13

My mom helps me do my homework. She helps me clean my room. She helps me do everything I need help with. My mom is like a friend to me in every way. Sometimes when she needs help, I help her. I help my family with things if they need something, and they do the same thing with me and my sister. I help my sister with homework and help her clean her room. She also helps me.
Heather Cotton, Age 8

There was a boy who couldn't talk or write. I taught him how to talk and write in cursive and regular.
Christian Johnson, Age 9

Giving makes me feel wonderful. Giving makes me feel good. Giving is to give something away that you really like.
Michael Moore, Age 11

I give stuff to people that I don't want anymore. I give clothes that I can't wearto people, and I give toys and things from my house to the poor.

It is nice to give people what you don't want and clothes that you can't wear. There are all kinds of things you can give. This makes me happy.
DJ Coffee, Age 8

My cousin Peter gave me a toy. It is called a Gali; it is a robot. I am going to give him a toy since he gave me one.

My friend gave me a Nintendo game. I gave him a Playstation game back.

Jesus died for our sins, so I will die, too, if I have to. I am a good person, and I will give my life too.
Taylor Rutland, Age 9

My mom and dad and nana gave me a lot of birthday presents. When they gave them to me, I was very, very happy. My presents were money and gift certificates, and to me that was really nice for them to do, especially on my birthday.
Savannah Tarpley, Age 9

I like giving because you can give stuff to people that you don't want but they do. You both win.
DJ Coffee, Age 8

Giving makes me happy. It makes me feel good when I give things. It makes them happy, and so am I too.
Savannah Casterline, Age 7

I give to my mom and dad and my sister. I give them love and care. I give them respect, and they give me respect and care. My mom and dad give me a place to live.
Charles Arms, Age 11

71

Giving is...

I share a golf club. I share golf balls. I share a pool stick. I share turns. I take turns. I share my toys. I share a game.

My friend gave me a toy. My mom gave me a Playstation. My dad gives me allowance. My granpa let me swim. My friend Dillon gave me a car. My Aunt gives me money. My dad bought me a dirt bike. My friends ride around with me.

Justin Currey, Age 11

I like giving. It makes me feel good. I like giving because my teacher gives us field trips. Today I gave my science teacher something for no reason. My family members give me presents. One time this man named Terrance from the A's gave me a ball that they had used.

Amanda Crispin, Age 10

Giving is something someone does or gives. We should be thankful for everything because everything we have is what someone gave you. Most of what you are God gave you, and you should be thankful. I know I am.

Olivia Preston, Age 12

I gave my friend a letter because she was very sick. When I gave her the letter, she read the letter and smiled.

Savannah Casterline, Age 7

I help my brother tie his shoes. I help Sharonese, my sister, open a bag of chips. I help wash dishes and clean up the house. I help cut grass and trim trees. I help do cars and bikes. I help cook some food. I help buy food and help shop for groceries. I help do chores.

Desiree Cantrell, Age 8

Chapter Five
Big Stories

Art by Emily Parsley

Lion Kind

Once there were three bunnies. They were very unfortunate. They hardly had any food. So they had to start taking just one nibble a day. One day they looked in their cabinet. "Oh no! There is no food left!" said one of the rabbits. So they set out on a search for carrots. On their journey it was very hot. They could not find any water! It was so hot they could not go seven inches more. So they lay down to catch their breath. As they were getting up, a lion approached them. It did not growl or try to bite them. It just gave them some carrots. The rabbits were trembling with fear. Finally one of the rabbits said "Thanks!" They all hopped to their hole, amazed at how the lion acted toward them. They were all really hungry. "Let's send something to the lion for his kindness and for giving," said the eldest one. And they had no troubles ever again. Especially with carrots.

Ali Deatherage, Age 8

Giving is...

I can give my time by volunteering at a senior citizens home or at the homeless shelter. By giving my time, skills, and presence, I give back to my community.

I give to my community to improve someone's way of life. When I give, I do not expect anything in return. I give just to help out those who are in need. Giving gives me joy and a sense of worth. Jesus gave His life so that I could live; now I give back my talents that He has provided to me.

Giving is not only fun and worthwhile, it is also my duty.

Tamyra Bradby (Ms. Tamyra), Staff

Once upon a time there was a lady named Mrs. Com, and she had a husband named Mr. Puter. Mrs. Com was a very nice lady and sweet, everybody said. There was a poor man on the other side of the street. He had a cup sitting in front of him. On the cup a sign said, "I NEED A HOME SOON FOR ME AND MY DAUGHTER." As Mrs. Com passed by, she thought about it in her head over and over again until she got home.

When she got home, her husband was already home. She told Mr. Puter about what she saw on the street. He was thinking about it, too. Then he said, "I'll work more overtime so that we can build a house for them." Mrs. Come thought that was a good idea. So the next day she went back to the same street and talked to the man, "My name is Luther Duracraft," he said. Mrs. Com left really quick. She went to fix lunch for her and Mr. Puter.

The next day, Mr. Puter got the money for the house. They called Hill's Construction. They said that the house would be done in six months. Mr. Puter said, "Okay, I'll see you then." Mrs. Com was so happy that she cried.

Eight months later, Mrs. Com was on her way to the street where Mr. Duracraft and his daughter were. She picked them up and took them to the million dollar house. Mr. Duracraft said, "How can I repay you?" Mrs. Com just looked at him and smiled.

Two years later, Mr. Duracraft pulled up to Mrs. Com's house and gave her $60.6 million for taking care of them for all those years. Mrs. Com just started to cry. She and her husband died on May 10, 1923.

Zarrina Wallace, Age 11

I gave my life up for my friends. My friends had gotten run over by a car. The man who hit them sent me on my spree to go get their parents. I risked my life by going as fast as I could while panicking. I went to the first house, and the mom thought I was playing. After she learned that I was serious, she was frightened. She had two little daughters and had to do something with them. She ran next door to see if her neighbors could babysit for a while, but they weren't home. So, she took them with her, and I took her to where her kid was. I had to go get the other parents. So I went out and she was real frightened too. I led her to where they were. Then the ambulance left and I went home. My parents took me to the hospital. It was sad to see my friends in a hospital bed. One of my friends broke his leg and the other one had to have air pumped into him and broke his leg. I felt sad until they came home. I used to go visit them at their houses all the time.
Chaisson Allen, Age 12

Giving is a very healthy thing to do. I don't give, but I see a lot of people who do it. I think that a lot of my friends and teachers are giving, but I never want them to give. Just as long as they show friendship.

When I was about seven, in church they talked about God giving His life for our sins. I think that God and Jesus are the most giving people on the earth. He gave me a life and I gave Him worship because I love Him more than anything. He's my father and my king. I love Him for who He is, not what people think of Him.
Briana Luchtefeld, Age 13

Martin Luther King Jr. fought for our freedom and our rights so blacks and whites could drink from the same water fountain and eat from the same table. So did Harriet Tubman. She gave her time to save other slaves. She got killed because she risked her life to save her family and her friends and probably people she didn't know. That is what giving is all about.
Liqa Minter, Age 12

Giving is...

Once upon a time there was a little girl named Goldilocks. She was supposed to go get some muffins to give to her mother. Then she saw some bears riding on these peoples' bikes. Then she saw a bear's house, so she went in the house because she saw food in it called porridge. She went in the bear's bed. She slept in the bear's bed. She said, "This bed is so bumpy." Then she went to another bear's bed, and said it was too soft. Then she went to the last bear's bed and it was just right. She slept and slept until the bears came home.

When the bears came home, she told them thank you for giving her food and a place to sleep. Then she went home.
Antoinette Jenkins, Age 8

God gave His only son to us to show us the way to eternal life. How can I help others find the light?

Well, here is the story to explain it. We should go to church to hear the Word, then become missionaries and give the Word to people who don't have the opportunity to go to church.

In the New Testament, it even tells us we should be missionaries.

We should follow Jesus and tell people about the gift of life from Jesus Christ. So accept Christ so you can have this gift of life.
Josh Hughey, Age 11

When I think of giving, it is hard for me not to write about someone who was not only giving to me, but to everyone who knew him. God was gracious enough to give me the privilege of knowing Bob Hayes. Bob was a man that touched everyone's lives around him. It did not matter how long you were around him, you would always remember him if you ever saw him again.

There is not a day that goes by that I don't think of him or wish that I could talk to him one last time. When Bob died, it was one of the hardest things I have ever had to face. Now that he is gone, I guess you can say that all of Bob's family and friends had to give him back to God so He could enjoy him like we did for the short time he was with us.
Clint Hickerson (Mr. Clint), Staff

One day there was a little boy and his name was Ryan. On Christmas he got a big stuffed doll that he already had from his aunt. He turned to his aunt and rudely said, "I already have this." That person was so mad, she had to leave the room. After the presents were handed out, the mom of his friend talked to him and told him that what he did was very rude and selfish. The boy felt so disappointed that he ran upstairs and told her he was so sorry.

The next day they took back the big stuffed animal that he got from the lady and got something else. The minute after he got home, he gave her a big hug and a kiss and apologized even more. She thought it was so sweet that she took him out for ice cream. He said "Thank you for everything." After that day, he was thankful for anything he got.

Yet he still felt disappointed about the way he acted towards his aunt. He felt it was just so rude and he wanted to get her something. So he took all of his allowance money and bought her a silver necklace. She was so happy, she gave him a big fat kiss. She explained to him why she was so mad: He acted so rude when he could have just said "thank you," waited until they were done, and then said kindly, "I already have this. Please take it and get something else." After that he told her he had learned his lesson.
Billy Richards, Age 12

Giving makes me proud to know that I am a true Christian. It makes me feel like a giving person. It makes me feel so good. I want to be very good at giving. It is real fun to give. There are poor people out in the world. It is sad to have no shelter, food or water. It is hard to survive outside in the world. It is good to be a giving person. This is a good time to give if you give to people. Not all people can learn about God and Jesus. This is a thing that you can do. It can help poor people. Give stuff you don't need to orphanages. This is a good world we live in. This is a way you can help – give money to poor people so they can learn about God.
Taylor Rutland, Age 9

Giving is...

Giving is something you should do because it is friendly. I like giving because it is great to be nice to people. Giving is like dreams coming true. If you give, it will come back to you, like God says. I like giving to other people because they are special and nice. I like helping people and giving them the things they need. Helping people is something everybody should do because it is being nice and respectful to people.

I know why people give: because they really enjoy giving to people because it is something everybody does to live. I really enjoy sharing with other people and like helping people who have no home and no clothes. Helping those kinds of people makes them very happy about getting things because they don't have those things.
Keywannia Pickett, Age 13

There are some countries that do not have a lot of stuff, if you ask me. In fact, there are some countries and states that go days, and maybe weeks, without water, or even food. Some children's parents have abandoned them so they have nowhere to go. Some children eat, sleep and play in trash that people dump. Those children are hungry, bored, and probably sleepy because they stay up at night to protect themselves and maybe their sisters and brothers or others that are lonely. To give is better than to receive. I have so much stuff, I don't know what to do with all of it. So, sometimes I give it to the Goodwill, the nursing home, or the Salvation Army. If you ask me, that is not the place for children, and not even adults. It's not a good place for anybody to have to live in my opinion. Usually people get made fun of because of living there. My best friend, Zach, lives in a huge house. He is my friend and he probably wouldn't make fun of me. There are thousands of people who need shelter and food, so always remember that giving is more important than receiving.

I give every day. I have a Spanish girl in my class who can barely speak English at all. She can say "thank you," "you're welcome," "sorry," and "bathroom." She can also type on a computer and read in English, but she doesn't know what it means. I help her when I can. Can you give every day? Sure you can!

Giving is better than receiving!
Jessica Wilson, age 12

The thing I most remember as a gift from someone is my skates. They are black, the wheels are rainbow, and the laces are really cool. They are also rainbow, but with fluorescent colors. I go skating almost every Friday.

The last time I went skating was on Sunday night, all night until 6:30 in the morning. I wear a size 6, and the skates hurt the right side of my feet because they are so wide.

I got them for Christmas. I've always wanted skates since I was seven years old. I've been skating since I was five years old. I got my skates at the Skate Center West. All fall and winter last year, I was begging for those skates. And I thank my dad because he got them for me.
Briana Luchtefeld, Age 12

A few days ago, Lenora got home from school, lay her stuff down, and ran to the message machine. She was expecting a message from her mom on her treatment. "Yes!" she thought. The button was blinking. She pushed it. Then a shudder went up her back. Her mother was diagnosed with lung cancer. The next few months, all Lenora did was take care of her mother. After a year and a half, her mother got cured. If you look at it the way I do, she gave a lot in a great time of need.
Lauren Walker, Age 12

Hello, my name is Bianca. I just moved here from Tallahassee, Florida. I go to a different school and I've been meeting new friends every day. My family's house is a big, beautiful light blue house. A while back, I met a young boy named Anthony. He wasn't a very intelligent boy, but he was very popular and was on the football team. I am a smart child myself, and I am in the 7th grade. Anthony is in the 8th grade.

Well, the other day he asked for my help because I guess he knew that I was a smart person. He asked me to help him with his homework. I like being nice, so I said that I would help him and show him how to do his work.

The boy now understands how to do the activities he was assigned to. This goes to show that giving is an important thing in life.
Jessica Walls, Age 13

Giving is...

What would you do if you had to feed over 2,000 boys and girls and didn't have any money or food?

One time there was no food at all for breakfast in Gladys Gardeners orphanage, and she had no money to buy any. She had the children all come in and sit down at the tables. Then she thanked God for their food, as she always did, but there was none. The tables were empty.

Suddenly, someone was at the door. There stood the baker. "I couldn't sleep last night," he said. "The Lord asked me to get up and bake you some bread for the children." There before their eyes was enough hot bread for everyone.

The bell rang again. Who do you think it was this time? The milkman. "My milk cart has broken down right in front of your orphanage. I would like to give you my cans of milk," he said.

Oh, what joy! God heard their prayers and had sent them breakfast.

Zarrina Wallace, age 11

This is a story about a boy that gives.

One day a boy wished he could have a new toy. His mom couldn't afford to buy it for him. The boy went into a strange forest. He had never been there. He went in a few miles and found an old house. He decided to go in. When he stepped on the deck, an old man came out. The boy was scared. The man said to the boy, "Come in and wish for whatever you want." The boy did. The boy wished for a brand new toy. The toy was a skateboard. Then he opened his eyes and it was there. The man said, "See there? It appeared in front of you." The boy said thank you then had to leave. "Bye," said the boy.

Dillon Sweeney, Age 10

This boy lost a pet. The next day he saw his dog dead on the road. He cried the whole day. He didn't know that someone was watching him. This person came the next day and left a puppy on the boy's doorstep. He left a card that said "From me to you."

Kayla Walker, Age 9

Once there was a lamb. He was walking in a pasture when all of the sudden he spotted a butterfly. He followed the butterfly until it finally flew away. He looked around and saw that he was nowhere near home. He started to cry. "Where am I?" he said to himself.

Suddenly, he heard someone crying. He followed the sound, and it led him to a little girl. "Why are you crying?" the lamb asked. "Because I can't find my way home," she said. "I can't find my way home either," he told her. "Well, where do you live?" the girl asked the lamb. "I live in Mr. Lincoln's pasture," the lamb said. "I live on Baker Street," said the girl. The lamb knew where Baker Street was – three blocks down on the left. The girl knew where Lincoln's pasture was – over the hill and under the fence. So they shared their ideas, and both found their way home and lived happily ever after.
Ali Deatherage, Age 8

Chapter Six
Random Thoughts

Art by Donann Melton

Giving to the earth is like recycling and stopping pollution. If you stop pollution, the earth will thank you. I love to help the earth. You will be surprised at what you can do.
Jessica Simons, Age 8

Giving is a gift of life. If you give, give, give you will live, live, live a happy life. People may give you presents, people may give you care, but never take for granted the gift God gives to you – His love.
Calvin French, Age 10

Giving is important. If someone is poor or homeless, you should give them shelter and food for them to live in a house so they can eat at night and in the morning.
DJ Coffee, Age 8

Giving is what you do to give nice things to people that need it. It's also what people do to be nice and thoughtful to people that desperately need it.

Giving is what you do to be nice and helpful. You do this to be nice and help other people. That's all!
Dallas Brobst, Age 11

Giving is something you do for your friends and family. It's better to give than to receive.
Charles Arms, Age 11

Giving is what you do when you help someone. Giving is a nice thing to do. People who get what you give to them appreciate what you have done for them.
Chaisson Allen, Age 12

Times get hard, things get rough,
We try our best to be strong and tough.
In times of need,
Powerful thought can help exceed
The love that's put into our heart
As we each take a different part.
Both love and hate
We scrape the slate
To help and love again.
To give is to feel,
To feel is to love.
The power of giving can explain.
It always will down any lane.
Ashley Hattabaugh, Age 13

Giving is...

Giving is a good thing to do. Making people happy, doing good stuff, enjoying stuff, and playing games with your friends are all kinds of giving.
Cassandra Peppers, Age 9

Giving is good because it is fun. When I give something to somebody, I hope they feel good because I feel good.
Alicia Todd, Age 8

Giving is fun. Last week someone gave me something and I enjoyed it. Yesterday I gave him back something. I like sharing. Giving is fun.
Jake Tarpley, Age 10

Giving is important. It is important to give and share because sharing is caring about other people. I am glad that I share and care.
Andy Swann, Age 7

It is very cool to give away toys and games. I was very happy when I gave away my toys and games. I was a little sad because I liked them still.

I would love to give money a lot more. I would love to give animals too.

Giving is nice. It's good and fun and very cool. It is a part of our world. Giving comes from the heart.
Travis Stanley, Age 8

I have given away my small clothes and my baby dolls to other kids. Giving toys to kids makes me feel like I take care of others. I give my time to help my sister too.
Samantha Spencer, Age 14

Each day we give our time, our talents, money and ourselves to something whether we are at home or at work. There is something we can give, but it doesn't cost any money and can be given over and over. I'm talking about a smile. Someone once said it takes more muscles to frown than it does to smile. This means I can use my muscles to keep smiling. A smile can be given away when you meet someone, and you won't believe how that changes someone's day. A smile can wipe away any tears of sadness that someone is feeling and restore any joy. A smile can be passed on from one person to the next. A smile keeps on giving and giving. So, the next time you meet someone, smile. You have received the best gift in the whole world and it is free. Thank you for smiling today.
Connie Smith (Ms. Connie), Staff

Giving is caring about people. It is a very good thing to do. It is important on Christmas. It would be a better world too if everyone gave all the time.

You would have a better heart if you gave.
Megan Sinvichith, Age 9

Giving is wonderful because you make someone else happy. I give my little sister love with a hug and a kiss. I got a little sister hug back. I like giving a lot.

Giving is inspiring. I pray for the poor or rich. I give the homeless people a blanket. One said thank you.

I feel good after giving.
Jessica Simons, Age 8

Giving makes me feel happy because it makes God happy too. I just love giving up stuff. I just hate snatching stuff from people. I will try more to be nice and give.

Helping Mother Nature is what I do to save the world and make God happy. I love it when God is happy.
Alex Scott, Age 9

Giving is...

One day my friends came over to my house. We made lemonade to have a lemonade stand. We made lots of money and we donated it to a homeless shelter.

One day I saved my money. When I saved it, I gave it to my mom because she gives all her money to me.

I had toys that I didn't want, so I gave my toys that I didn't want to my friend.

Cristie Sanborn, Age 9

Chapter Seven
Holidays

Art by Calvin French

I love Christmas. It is very fun to receive gifts, especially the ones you really want. It is also fun to see all of your family so happy.
Nikki Trice, Age 13

I was given lots of things for Christmas. I got some candy, some toys and a necklace from my granny.
Brooke Duke, Age 9

Giving is...

My mom and dad gave me a three-wheeler, a bike, a racing bike and a CD for Christmas.
Chris Bush, Age 12

Giving is something that everybody does on Christmas and Valentine's Day. Things you give to other people can be presents, candy, cards or money.
John Bucy, Age 10

What I got for Christmas is my own Nintendo 64, a BB gun, and a remote control truck.
Dallas Brobst, Age 11

What I got for Christmas is a toy. But that doesn't matter. It is your family and friends and the nice hearts inside of us that matter.
Sam Loyd, Age 8

Santa gave me a fish tank, a radio, a CD and a pet cat.
Julia Jones, Age 9

Santa gave me a small sun for Christmas. It made me feel happy.
Tyler Hall, Age 7

For Christmas I got a scooter, a telescope, clothes and a big tiger blanket.
Halee Gregory, Age 9

Last year for Christmas I got a scooter and so did my brother. We also got an autographed Tennessee Titans football. I got a remote control car and gave it away to someone.
Kyle Goolesby, Age 11

Santa gave me a new house.
Hillary Garrett, Age 9

For Christmas last year, my family was in great cheer when it was time for presents. I was excited; and when the wrapper came off, my eyes were delighted to see the very best present of all.
Hali Garrett, Age 13

Santa Claus gave me a Nelly CD, a color Gameboy, a Crash Bash, and Mortal Combat.
Majlik Roach, Age 10

I got Digimon, Pokémon, movies, puzzles, and cars too. But most of all I got love.
Austin Poteete, Age 8

Santa Claus gave me perfume, candy, lip-gloss, and notes about the milk and cookies I leave him every Christmas Eve.
Emily Parsley, Age 8

Giving is about gratefulness, birds in the nest, and Christmas presents. It's not about being lonely. It's the very best. Just pass the test. I don't think I could fail a test. PlayStation 2 is usually the best.
Mike Oden, Age 13

My grandfather gives me a lot of stuff. On Christmas we go over to my cousins' house and have a lot of fun. We have good food there every Friday. We go to the golf place and ride Go Karts. We went there two times. The second time my cousins crashed. When we left, we got donuts. My cousin Nick goes with me, and we do golf and bumper boats too.
Darien Jackson, Age 8

Giving is...

Giving is like Thanksgiving. When you see a homeless person on the streets asking if you can you spare some change, even if you don't know them, you can give them some pennies or something. Like the good Lord said, if you give something, good will turn out. So, when I see somebody who needs something, even if it is three dollars or so, I give it to them because something good will happen.
Liqa Minter, Age 12

Giving is fun. I like to give. I give presents on Christmas. I give hugs on Thanksgiving. I give toys to the homeless.
Austin Mersinger, Age 10

I got a hat for Christmas and I got some movies too. I can't forget the cool games I got. I had fun.
Drew Woodard, Age 8

It feels good when someone gives to me. When we get something, we should give back. It would be nice. Someone gave me some school supplies, a pair of shoes and some other cool things.

For Christmas there are a lot of things I want. But I need to ask to get something. If I get something I want, I should be thankful and try to give something back.
Ashley Woodard, Age 11

Giving is special on holidays. It makes me happy. I love giving. I like to give my toys.
James Williams, Age 9

Giving is something you do for friends and family. Like the Christmas saying goes, "It's better to give than receive."
Justin White, Age 13

Giving is really important to everybody. When you give, you have really been blessed by God. God is happy when you give to another person. When you give, you will receive. I give to a lot of people every Christmas. I feel so wonderful when I give, and you will too. I know you will feel the same way. All of my family members give to some of the people.
Zarrina Wallace, Age 11

Chapter Eight
Tragedy

I would give food and clothes to New York and help them raise money to rebuild the twin buildings and hire new workers. I would feel good about giving something instead of receiving.
Jessica Wilson, Age 11

Give the Red Cross blood for the people who really need it.
Kayla Walker, Age 9

Giving is a good thing. I would give to people in New York. It would really help them a lot, and they would really like it that I cared. I would feel really good about it.
Derrick Ferguson, Age 13

Giving is a good thing. You give every single day. I feel sorry for the people that died on Tuesday, September 11, 2001. God will give them peace.
Amanda Crispin, Age 10

Giving is a wonderful thing. You can give almost anything. You can give money or your homework to the teacher. You can give presents to people on their birthday or Christmas or any time. You can give whatever you want to anybody if you want to. You can give to me, you can give to her or him. You can give anyone anything. You can just give for fun or to be nice to people. I give my mom help if she wants it from me.

You can be like the Red Cross. They are giving blood and clothes because of the plane that crashed into a building that killed a lot of people and destroyed homes and stuff. I did not watch the whole thing. It was scary.
Samantha Davis, Age 12

Giving is a good thing to do. We should try to help the people who were in the accident by giving blood, food, clothes and medicine. Just thank God for the people who survived. We should thank the people who gave blood. The people who are still alive were lucky. Everyone is special.
Makita Batey, Age 9

I really like to give now because of what had happened. If I were there, I think I would go in and risk my life for all those people. I really think that I've learned a lesson, and this has changed my life. I pray more for my family now because of this situation. Life has changed, but I accept it because kids have to go through things like that. This mostly goes back to giving my life for those people. I thank God for the ones that survived and went to heaven with Him.
Briana Luchtefeld, Age 12

You can give donations to the Red Cross, because now they really need blood and medical supplies. Because of the D.C. and New York crashes, I think people should give. My mom gave blood, and it made me feel good that we were able to help.
Katie Lower, Age 11

I give my heart and soul to all the people that died. My dog went through a lot. She almost got run over by a car two times. I give her my trust, my heart and my love. If my parents were not here, I do not know what I would do because I love my family. I am glad we don't live in New York.
Stephen Price, Age 10

My family went to the Red Cross and gave blood because we felt sad for the people that lost loved ones in New York. They lost aunts and grandparents. God bless the USA. God bless New York. My prayers go out to all the people that lost loved ones.
Clinton McClendon, 16

Giving is...

I like to give. If more people would give, our world could come together as one.
DeAndrea Mack, Age 12

I hate to see bad things happen to people, and I always try to give something.

I will give my life for this country.

I would give blood for those who need it in the World Trade Center, but I am too young.

The WTC has been hit by planes. Both towers fell down on September 11. The first one fell down at 9:20 a.m. The second one fell down at 9:45 a.m. It was a day of terror. This is not just any terrorist act – it could be the start of a war.
Seth Woods, Age 9

The thing that happened on September 11, 2001 was the most horrible day of our lives. We cried and we got mad. But we all knew that we would give love and not hate.
Kayla Walker, Age 9

We should give blood to those who were hurt when the Trade Center got hit. We should give food and drinks to those people who cannot buy food. I feel good when someone is smiling. I give clothing to the poor and foster kids. We should help all people.
Nick Warren, Age 11

Giving is a good thing, and that's what God put us on the earth for us to learn about. Tuesday was not a very respectful or giving day. But then again a lot of people helped each other get out of that building. Now I've heard a lot of other stories about getting out, like how a man helped a lady in a wheelchair get down a staircase. I also learned that giving your life for more than one is worth it. That's what I call giving.
Briana Luchtefeld, Age 12

Afterword

Giving represents many things. In the Bible, one in six verses in Matthew, Mark and Luke mentions giving.

God owns everything. John the Baptist said a man can receive nothing except it be given him from Heaven. Every good gift and every perfect gift is from above and comes from the Father.

Giving is a strategy. Raise a child in the way he should go and when he is old, he will not depart from it, we are reminded from Proverbs. Our greatest giving should be into the lives of people, an eternal investment.

The Gallup pollsters report that the percentage of giving to charitable causes actually declines with the increase in household income. But, giving is more than about money. In my opinion, it is about obedience to God. We are reminded, "Behold, to obey is better than to sacrifice."

In God's economy, giving is about discipline. God has not obligated Himself to bless anything except our obedience. We should excel in the grace of giving. Again, from the Bible we are told, "...abound in everything, in faith and utterance and knowledge, and in all diligence, and in your love to us, see that you abound in this grace also."

Giving is an expression of thankfulness. Every man according as he purposes in his heart, so let him give, not grudgingly, or of necessity, for God loves a cheerful giver. Give and it shall be given unto you.

Giving allows us to look beyond ourselves. Abundant living comes from abundant giving. Giving determines what God can do in our lives.

The Jordan River flows with millions of gallons of water, but the Dead Sea always remains the same. Nothing living can survive there either. God's grace, mercy and patience flow into our lives, and we must let them flow through to others. It will brighten our spirit and brighten the lives of others.

Steve McKinney
Executive Director
Boys & Girls Clubs

About the Boys & Girls Clubs

Our Mission is to inspire and enable all young people, especially those from disadvantaged circumstances, to realize their full potential as productive, responsible and caring citizens.

This mission is reinforced by our core beliefs, which are that Clubs provide: a safe place to learn and grow; ongoing relationships with caring, adult professionals; life-enhancing programs and character development experiences; and hope and opportunity.

Board of Directors
2001

INDEX

Printed in the United States
2542